Country Hotels

 teNeues

Publisher: Paco Asensio
Editor: Haike Falkenberg
Editorial coordination and introduction: Ana G. Cañizares
Documentation: Lars Oscenda
Art director: Mireia Casanovas Soley
Layout: Gisela Legares Gili
German translation: Haike Falkenberg/Lars Osceda
French translation: Michel Ficerai
Spanish translation: Marta Casado Lorenzo

Published in the US and Canada by
teNeues Publishing Company
16 West 22nd Street, New York, N.Y. 10010, USA
Tel.: 001-212-627-9090, Fax: 001-212-627-9511

Published in Germany, Austria and Switzerland by
teNeues Verlag GmbH + Co KG
Am Selder 37, 47906 Kempen, Germany
Tel.: 0049-(0)2152-916-0, Fax: 0049-(0)2152-916-111

Published in the UK and Ireland by
teNeues Publishing Uk Ltd.
Aldwych House, 71/91 Aldwych
London WC2B 4HN, UK

www.teneues.com

ISBN: 3-8238-5574-3

Editorial project:

©2002 LOFT Publications
Domènech, 9 2-2
08012 Barcelona, Spain
Tel.: 0034 93 218 30 99
Fax.: 0034 93 237 00 60
e-mail:loft@loftpublications.com
www.loftpublications.com

If you would like to suggest projects for inclusion in our next
volumes, please e-mail details to us at:loft@loftpublications.com

Die Deutsche Bibliothek – CIP-Einheitsaufnahme
Ein Titeldatensatz für diese Publikation ist bei der Deutschen
Bibliothek erhältlich.

Printed by: Gràfiques Ibèria S.A, Barcelona, Spain

March 2002

Taking a holiday can mean very different things for different people. For some it is simply a way of breaking away from the monotony and stress of daily life and work. For others it is a far more contemplated agenda in which there is a search for a very specific setting and mood that tailors to their wants and needs.

More and more people are flocking from the city in pursuit of a place to get away. The world's favorite cities are no longer the most-wanted holiday destination for the majority of weekend travellers. There is an ever-growing necessity to have a greater contact with nature to distract us from the urban setting in which we have grown so accustomed to live in. Nature reminds us of who we are as human beings and somehow helps us to put our lives into perspective, and this effect is crucial to relax both body and mind. It is for this reason that the perfect hotel does not just amount to a basket of fancy toiletries and luxury services, but has become a place personalized to cater to particular clients who seek to indulge their senses. Hotels situated on the countryside offer a unique experience for its guests, most importantly because of their stunning surroundings and picturesque landscapes. They also provide the opportunity for guests to enjoy activities only possible on these locations, such as horse-back riding, canoeing, skiing, and camping. Others specialize in pampering their priveleged visitors with spa treatments, thermal baths and exquisite regional cuisine. These destinations can serve as an alternative work place, a romantic hideaway, a peaceful retreat, a reunion for friends, or simply a breath-taking refuge.

COUNTRY HOTELS brings together a selection of hotels, inns, posadas, lodges, villas and mansions from all around the world that impress with their heavenly surroundings and their remarkable services. Some are brand new constructions designed by important architects and others dating back several hundred years have been thoughtfully decorated by expert interior designers. Still others are more modest havens that are no less exceptional for their personalized hospitality and extraordinary location. Anywhere from a luxury ski resort on the East Coast, to a 17th century Tuscan villa, to a five-cabin fishing lodge tucked away in the lush marshlands of Argentina, the variety of country hotels offered here leaves any keen traveller spoiled for choice. In sum, a jaw-dropping compilation that will quickly turn envy into an irresistable desire to return to nature in the comfort of some of the most beautiful hotels in the world.

Urlaub zu machen, hat für verschiedene Leute sehr unterschiedliche Bedeutungen. Für einige ist es lediglich ein Weg, aus der Monotonie und dem Stress des Alltags auszubrechen. Andere sehen darin ein weit umfangreicheres Unterfangen, das ihren Wünschen und Bedürfnissen in Bezug auf eine bestimmte Umgebung und Stimmung genau entsprechen soll.

In Scharen strömen die Menschen aus der Stadt und suchen einen Ort, an den sie sich zurückziehen können. Die großen Weltstädte haben inzwischen ihren Rang als beliebteste Reiseziele für den Großteil der Wochenend ausflügler abgetreten. Um von der urbanen Umgebung abzulenken, hat sich ein stetig zunehmendes Bedürfnis nach direkterem Kontakt mit der Natur entwickelt, die den Städter daran erinnert, dass er ein Mensch ist, und ihm hilft, dem Leben eine Perspektive zu geben. Gerade dieser Einfluss erlaubt, Körper und Geist zu entspannen. Daher zeichnet sich das perfekte Hotel nicht durch exklusive Toilettenartikel und luxuriöse Handtücher aus, sondern ist zu einem auf den einzelnen Menschen ausgerichteten Ort geworden, der den sinnlichen Bedürfnissen individueller Kunden gerecht wird. Hotels auf dem Land bieten ihren Gästen aufgrund ihrer malerischen Landschaften einzigartige Erlebnisse. Sie ermöglichen Aktivitäten, die man nur an solchen Orten in vollen Zügen genießen kann, wie beispielsweise Reiten, Kanu oder Ski fahren und Erkundungen in die überraschendsten Winkel. Andere haben sich auf das Verwöhnen ihrer Gäste mit Thermalbädern, Wellness-Behandlungen und einer exquisiten regionalen Küche spezialisiert. Diese Reiseziele dienen als Ausweich-Arbeitsplatz, sind romantisches Versteck, friedvolle Oase, Treffpunkt mit Freunden oder einfach atemberaubender Zufluchtsort.

COUNTRY HOTELS stellt Hotels, Inns, Posadas, Lodges, Villen und herrschaftliche Landhäuser der ganzen Welt vor, die durch ihre bemerkenswerte Lage und ihren hervorragenden Service bestechen. Es sind moderne Neubauten bekannter Architekten, Jahrhunderte alte, von erfahrenen Innenarchitekten umsichtig dekorierte Gebäude oder schlichte Oasen, exzeptionell aufgrund ihrer herzlichen Gastfreundschaft und außergewöhnlichen Umgebung. Vom luxuriösen Ski-Resort an der amerikanischen Ostküste, über eine toskanische Villa aus dem 17. Jahrhundert bis hin zu einem nur fünf Hütten umfassenden Anglerparadies versteckt im argentinischen Marschland - die vorgestellten Landhotels stellen jeden unternehmungslustigen Reisenden vor die Qual der Wahl. Die anregende Zusammenstellung ruft schnell ein unwiderstehliches Verlangen beim Leser hervor, in die Natur zurück zu kehren und den Komfort einiger der schönsten Hotels der Welt zu genießen.

Nous avons tous notre conception très personnelle des vacances. Pour certains, c'est simplement un moyen de rompre la monotonie et le stress de la vie et du travail quotidiens. Pour d'autres, il s'agit d'un rendez-vous très attendu, objet d'une attention toute particulière en quête d'un décor et d'une atmosphère épousant parfaitement désirs et besoins.

De plus en plus de gens fuient la ville à la recherche d'un lieu d'évasion. Les cités phares internationales ne sont plus la destination de vacance privilégiée de la majorité des voyageurs en week-end. Est née une nécessité, sans cesse grandissante, d'entrer plus profondément en contact avec la nature, afin de se distraire du décor urbain qui nous est devenu si familier. La nature nous rappelle notre humanité et, d'une certaine façon, nous aide à mettre nos vies en perspective. Il s'agit là d'un élément essentiel pour soulager corps et âme. Pour cette raison, l'hôtel parfait n'est pas contenu tout entier dans un panier d'articles de toilettes et de services de luxe. Il est devenu un lieu personnalisé destiné à accueillir des clients particuliers cherchant à donner libre cours à leurs sens. Les hôtels situés à la campagne proposent une expérience unique à leurs hôtes, principalement en raison de leur cadre saisissant et de leurs paysages si pittoresques. Ils offrent également à leurs invités l'occasion de participer à des activités réservées à ces lieux, comme la randonnée équestre, le canoë, le ski ou le camping. D'autres tendent à choyer leurs visiteurs privilégiés avec des cures de thalassothérapie dans des sources thermales sans oublier une délicieuse cuisine régionale. Ces destinations peuvent ainsi offrir un cadre de travail alternatif, un nid romantique, une retraite tranquille, un lieu de réunion entre amis ou simplement un refuge merveilleux.

COUNTRY HOTELS vous présente une sélection d'hôtels, auberges, posadas, gîtes, villas et demeures tout autour du monde, impressionnant par leur décor paradisiaque et leurs services remarquables. Certains constituent des projets entièrement nouveaux, œuvres d'architectes de renom. D'autres, plusieurs fois centenaires, ont vu leur décoration remise avec soin au goût du jour par des experts en design d'intérieur. D'autres enfin proposent un havre, certes plus modeste, mais sans pour autant oublier leur hospitalité personnalisée et leur situation extraordinaire. D'une station de ski sur la côte Est à une villa toscane du XVIIème, en passant par un simple gîte de pêche à cinq chalets au cœur des luxuriants marais argentins, la diversité des hôtels ici dépeints laisse l'embarras du choix au voyageur. En fait, c'est tout un florilège captivant qui vous communiquera rapidement le désir irrésistible de revenir à la nature, dans le cadre confortable de quelques-uns des plus beaux hôtels du monde.

Tomarse unas vacaciones puede tener muchos significados, dependiendo de las personas. Para algunos es simplemente una manera de romper con la monotonía y el estrés de la vida diaria y el trabajo. Para otros, es algo más elaborado, una búsqueda de los lugares y detalles que más se ajustan a sus deseos y necesidades.

Cada vez más gente huye de las urbes en busca de un lugar de descanso. Las ciudades más grandes del mundo ya no son los destinos turísticos más solicitados por la mayoría de los viajeros de fin de semana. Existe una necesidad creciente de tener un mayor contacto con la naturaleza para distraernos de los núcleos urbanos en los que hemos nacido y en los que estamos tan acostumbrados a vivir. La naturaleza nos recuerda quiénes somos como seres humanos, de alguna manera nos ayuda a dotar a nuestras vidas de una perspectiva, y este efecto es crucial para relajar tanto el cuerpo como la mente. Por esta razón, el hotel perfecto no es aquel que dispone de los servicios más lujosos, sino el que atiende las necesidades de unos clientes que buscan mimar sus sentidos. Los hoteles situados en el campo ofrecen una experiencia única para sus huéspedes, sobre todo si se tienen en cuenta sus magníficos alrededores y sorprendentes paisajes. Además, brindan la oportunidad de desarrollar actividades que sólo se pueden llevar a cabo en estos lugares, como equitación, piragüismo, esquí o acampada. Otros se especializan en mimar a sus visitantes con tratamientos de salud y belleza, baños termales y una exquisita cocina regional. Estos destinos pueden servir como lugar alternativo de trabajo, escapada romántica, retiro pacífico, una reunión con amigos o, simplemente, un impresionante refugio.

COUNTRY HOTELS reúne una selección de hoteles, paradores, posadas, casas señoriales y mansiones de todo el mundo que impresionan por sus espectaculares alrededores y sus extraordinarios servicios. Algunos de ellos son de nueva construcción y han sido diseñados por importantes arquitectos; otros datan de hace cientos de años y han sido cuidadosamente decorados por expertos interioristas. Y otros, más modestos, no son menos excepcionales gracias a su trato personal y extraordinaria localización. Desde un complejo para esquiadores en la Costa Este hasta una villa del siglo XVII en la Toscana o un pequeño albergue de pescadores en las exóticas marismas de Argentina, la variedad de hoteles ofrecida es tal, que el viajero tendrá difícil la elección. En suma, se trata de una incomparable compilación que convertirá rápidamente la envidia en deseo irresistible de volver a la naturaleza encarnada en algunos de los hoteles más bellos del mundo.

WHEATLEIGH

ARCHITECT:	Tsao & McKown
CONSTRUCTION DATE:	1893
OPENING DATE:	2000
ADDRESS:	Hawthorne Road
	Lenox, Massachusetts 01240. USA
TEL.:	+ 1 413 637-0610
FAX:	+ 1 413 637-4507
	info@wheatleigh.com
	www.wheatleigh.com
ROOMS:	19 suites
SERVICES:	Restaurant, bar, phone, cable TV, CD, library, gym, meeting facilities, wedding facilities
PHOTOGRAPHER:	Roger Casas

GLENDORN HOTEL

OPENING DATE:	1995
ADDRESS:	1032 West Craydon Street
	Bradford, Pennsylvania 16701. USA
TEL.:	+ 1 800 843 8568
FAX:	+ 1 814 368 9923
	glendorn@glendorn.com
	www.glendorn.com
ROOMS:	6 cabins
SERVICES:	Restaurant, bar, phone, fax, en suite fireplaces, common game rooms
PHOTOGRAPHER:	Roger Casas

ACQUA HOTEL

ARCHITECT:	Ramon Zambrano
INTERIOR DESIGNER:	Marni Leis
OPENING DATE:	August 1999
ADDRESS:	555 Redwood Highway
	Mill Valley, California 94941. USA
TEL.:	+1 415 380 0400, Reservations: +1 888 662 9555
FAX:	+1 415 380 9696
	ccantu@jdvhospitality.com
	www.acquahotel.com
ROOMS:	50 guestrooms, including 25 junior suites
SERVICES:	Complimentary deluxe continental breakfast, state of the art phone system, CD, video, video and CD library, cable TV, air conditioning, fitness room, laundry, convention space
PHOTOGRAPHER:	Cesar Rubio

THE MILL HOUSE INN

ARCHITECT:	Steven Capaldo
OPENING DATE:	1996
ADDRESS:	31 North Main Street
	East Hampton, New York 11937. USA
TEL./FAX:	+ 1 631 324 9766
	innkeeper@millhouseinn.com
	www.millhouseinn.com
ROOMS:	8 doubles
SERVICES:	Restaurant, bar, phone, fax.
SPECIAL FEATURES:	Voted "America's Most Beautiful Village" in US and known for its spectacular ocean beaches
PHOTOGRAPHER:	Roger Casas

LAKE PLACID LODGE

CONSTRUCTION DATE:	1882
OPENING DATE:	1946, re-opened 1994
ADDRESS:	Whiteface Inn Road
	Lake Placid, New York 12946. USA
TEL.:	+ 1 518 523 2700
FAX:	+ 1 518 523 1124
	kathryn@lakeplacidlodge.com
	www.lakeplacidlodge.com
ROOMS:	17 rooms and suites
SERVICES:	Restaurant, bar, breakfast, guides, excursions, fishing, golf course, trailing, scenic flights
SPECIAL FEATURES:	Located in the Adirondack mountains, the most ancient known rocks in the world. Whitewater rafting, hiking and biking
PHOTOGRAPHER:	Roger Casas

WATERS EDGE HOTEL

ARCHITECT:	Ramon Zambrano
INTERIOR DESIGNER:	Marni Leis
OPENING DATE:	August 2000
ADDRESS:	25 Main Street
	Tiburon, California 94920. USA
TEL.:	+1 415 789 5999
FAX:	+1 415 789 5888
	ccantu@jdvhospitality.com
	www.acquahotel.com/waters_guestrooms.html
ROOMS:	23 guestrooms, including 2 suites
SERVICES:	Complimentary deluxe continental beakfast, state of the art phone system, CD player, video, video + CD library, cable TV, air conditioning, fitness room

THE POINT

OPENING DATE:	1986
ADDRESS:	PO Box 1327
	Saranac Lake, New York 12983. USA
TEL.:	+ 1 800 255 3530 or +1 518 891 5674
FAX:	+ 1 518 891 1152
	info@thepointresort.com
	www.thepointresort.com
ROOMS:	11 doubles
SERVICES:	Restaurant, bar, breakfast, spacious bath, lake view, private fireplace
SPECIAL FEATURES:	The Point was originally Camp Wonondra, the home of William Avery Rockefeller
PHOTOGRAPHER:	Roger Casas

THE INN AT SAW MILL FARM

ARCHITECT:	Rodney Williams Sr.
OWNER:	Rodney Williams Jr.
INTERIOR DESIGNER:	Ione Williams
OPENING DATE:	1968
ADDRESS:	Route 100 & Crosstown Road
	Box 367, West Dover, Vermont 05356. USA
TEL.:	+ 1 800 493 1133 or + 1 802 464 8131
FAX:	+1 802 464 1130
	sawmill@sover.net
	www.theinnatsawmillfarm.com
ROOMS:	21 doubles, including cottages and suites
SERVICES:	Restaurant, bar, phone, fax, fireplace, outdoor tennis court, swimming pool, canoe, trout ponds
PHOTOGRAPHER:	Roger Casas

Posada Agua Verde

Construction date:	1996
Address:	Road to San Carlos, 7.5 km from La Barra de Maldonado, on the hill Eguzquiza. Uruguay
Tel.:	+ 59 842 470 302
Fax:	+ 59 842 469 941
Rooms:	4 doubles, 2 suites
Services:	Phone, fax, restaurant
Special features:	Colonial style, lounges, swimming pool, horseback riding
Photographer:	Ricardo Labougle, Victor Carro

CARAVANSERAI

ARCHITECT:	Mathieu Boccara
INTERIOR DESIGNER:	Mathieu Boccara and Max Lawrence
CONSTRUCTION DATE:	2001
ADDRESS:	Caravanserai
	264 Ouled Ben Rahmoune, Marrakesh. Morocco
TEL.:	+ 212 44 30 03 02
FAX:	+ 212 44 30 02 62
	caravanserai@iam.net.ma
	www.caravanserai-marrakesh.com
ROOMS:	7 rooms and 10 suites
SERVICES:	Breakfast, bar, fax, phone, e-mail, private pools and terraces, hammam, massage, horse-riding, excursions
SPECIAL FEATURES:	Located in simple mud village overlooking palm groves of Marrakesh and High Atlas Mountains; hotel made out of traditional, organic and local materials
PHOTOGRAPHER:	Pere Planells

TIGMI TAGADERT

ARCHITECT:	Max Lawrence
INTERIOR DESIGNER:	Max Lawrence
OPENING DATE:	2002
ADDRESS:	Village de Tafadert,
	Haouz, Marrakesh. Morocco
TEL.:	+ 44 1380 828533, + 212 61 134422
FAX:	+ 44 1380 828630
	riadmabrouka@wanadoo.net.ma
	www.morocco-travel.com
ROOMS:	6 suites
SERVICES:	Gardens, pool, dining room, terraces, meals included
PHOTOGRAPHER:	Pere Planells

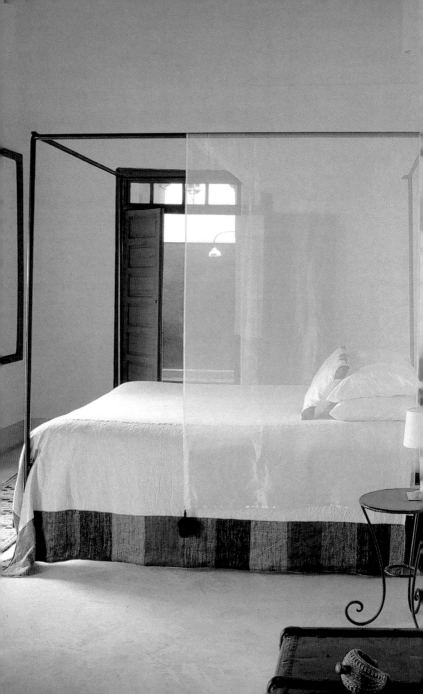

BABINGTON HOUSE

OWNER:	Soho House Country
CONSTRUCTION DATE:	14th-18th century
OPENING DATE:	1997
ADDRESS:	Babington
	NR Frone, Somerset BA11 3RW. UK
TEL.:	+ 44 1373 812266
FAX:	+ 44 1373 812112
	enquiries@babingtonhouse.co.uk
	www.babingtonhouse.co.uk.com
ROOMS:	27 doubles
SERVICES:	Restaurant, bar, wide-screen TV, DVD, Hifi, phone, fax, Italian design furniture
SPECIAL FEATURES:	Movie theater, gym, sauna, swimming pool, outdoor sports, three bedroom gate lodge
PHOTOGRAPHER:	Gunnar Knechtel

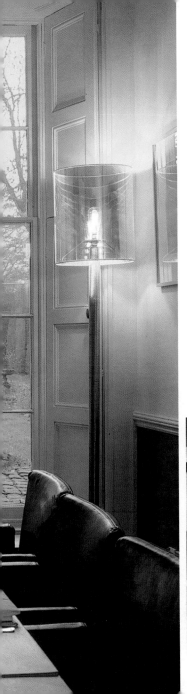

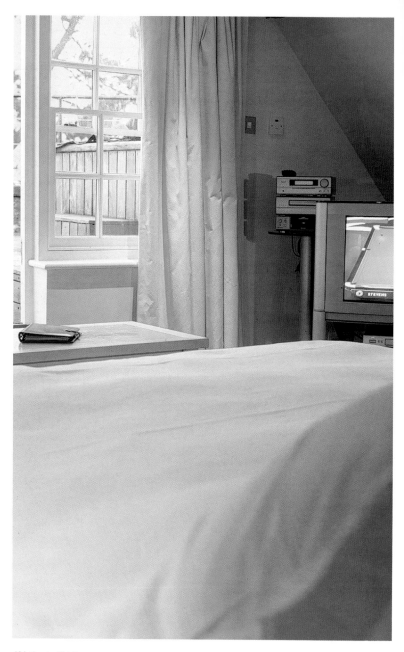

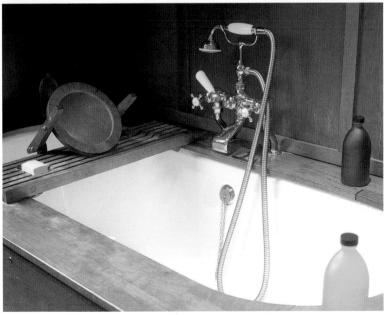

Nossa Senhora da Asunção Posada

<table>
<tr><td>ARCHITECT:</td><td>José Paolo Santos</td></tr>
<tr><td>OPENING DATE:</td><td>1997</td></tr>
<tr><td>ADDRESS:</td><td>Posada Nossa Senhora da Asunção
Apartado 61, 7040 909 Arriolos. Portugal</td></tr>
<tr><td>TEL.:</td><td>+ 351 26 641 9340, + 351 26 641 9365</td></tr>
<tr><td>FAX:</td><td>+ 351 26 641 9280</td></tr>
<tr><td>ROOMS:</td><td>32</td></tr>
<tr><td>SERVICES:</td><td>Restaurant, bar, phone, fax, air conditioning, swim-</td></tr>
</table>

Casal de Dama

OPENING DATE: 1998
ADDRESS: Toxofal de Cima, 2530, Lourinhã. Portugal
TEL.: + 351 261 411 053
FAX: + 351 261 423 200
casaldama.turismo@mail.telepac.pt
www.maisturismo.pt
ROOMS: 1 double, 3 singles
SERVICES: Bar, snack bar, swimming pool, parking, tennis court
PHOTOGRAPHER: Pep Escoda

POSADA FLOR DA ROSA

ARCHITECT:	Carrilho da Graça
OPENING DATE:	1995
ADDRESS:	Posada Flor da Rosa
	7430 999 Crato. Portugal
TEL.:	+ 351 24 599 7210
FAX:	+ 351 24 599 7212
ROOMS:	24 doubles
SERVICES:	Restaurant, bar, breakfast, phone, fax, air conditioning
PHOTOGRAPHER:	Pep Escoda

QUINTA DO JUNCAL

ARCHITECT:	Manuel Morgado
INTERIOR DESIGNER:	Ana Isabel Domingos
CONSTRUCTION DATE:	1890, recently restored
ADDRESS:	Serra D´El Rey
	2525 Serra D´El Rey, Peniche. Portugal
TEL.:	+351 262 905 030
FAX:	+351 262 905 301
	www.maisturismo.pt/qjuncal
ROOMS:	8 rooms and 3 cabins
SERVICES:	Gift shop, swimming pool, tennis court, driving range, hiking, historical, cultural and gastronomic circuits
PHOTOGRAPHER:	Pep Escoda

Quinta Do Hilario

Construction date	18th century
Opening date:	1997
Address:	Quinta Do Hilario
	2900, Setubal. Portugal
Tel.:	+ 351 26 553 8680
Fax:	+ 351 26 555 1682
	webmaster@quinta-hilario.net
	www.quinta-hilario.net
Rooms:	4 independent suites
Services:	Bar, phone, satellite TV, pavillion, swimming pool, orange groves
Photographer:	Pep Escoda

PALACIO SETEAIS

CONSTRUCTION DATE:	18th century
OPENING DATE:	1996
ADDRESS:	Rua Barbosa du Bocage, 8-10
	Sintra, 2710. Portugal
TEL.:	+ 351 21 923 3200
FAX:	+ 351 21 923 4277
	hpsetais@mail.telepac.et
ROOMS:	30
SERVICES:	Restaurant, bar, cable TV, laundry service, safe,
	baby-sitting, swimming pool, parking
PHOTOGRAPHER:	Pep Escoda

Quinta Do Campo

ARCHITECT:	Teresa Nunes da Ponte (reconstruction)
CONSTRUCTION DATE:	12th century, reconstructed in the 19th century
OPENING DATE:	1991, amplification 1994
ADDRESS:	Rua Carles O'Neill nº 20
	2450-801 Valado dos Frades. Portugal
TEL.:	+ 351 262 577 135
FAX:	+ 351 262 577 555
	quintadocampo@mail.telepac.pt
	www.quintadocampo.com
ROOMS:	8 doubles and 7 suites
SEVICES:	Restaurant, self-service bar, cable TV, laundry, library, indoor games, gardens and pedestrian circuits, bicycles, 4 wheel motorbikes
PHOTOGRAPHER:	Pep Escoda

RIDERS PALACE

ARCHITECT:	René Meierhofer
OPENING DATE:	2001
ADDRESS:	Riders Palace
	7032 Laax. Switzerland
TEL.:	+ 41 81 927 9700
FAX:	+ 41 81 927 9701
	riderspalace@alpenarena.ch
	www.riderspalace.ch
ROOMS:	71
SERVICES:	Restaurant, bar, night club featuring Ministry of Sound, digital entertainment, sports and social activities
SPECIAL FEATURES:	The first High-Tech hotel in the Alps
PHOTOGRAPHER:	Gaudenz Danuser

Pira Lodge

ARCHITECT:	Pablo Sanchez Elia
INTERIOR DESIGNER:	Laura Orcoyen
CONSTRUCTION DATE:	December 2000
ADDRESS:	Pasaje de "El Boqueron"
	Mercedes, Provincia de Corrientes. Argentina
TEL.:	+ 54 1143 3197 10
FAX:	+ 54 3773 4203 99
	info@piralodge.com
	www.piralodge.com
ROOMS:	5 doubles
SERVICES:	Restaurant, bar, air conditioning
SPECIAL FEATURES:	Kayaking, fly fishing, horseback riding
PHOTOGRAPHER:	Virginia del Giudice

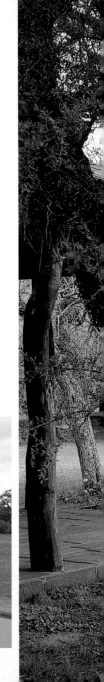

Estancia Ancón

Construction Date:	1933
Opening date:	2000
Address:	San José, Tupungato
	Provincia de Mendoza. Argentina
Tel./Fax:	+ 54 2622 488 245
	estanciancon@yahoo.com.ar
Rooms:	5 doubles
Services:	Horseback riding, visits to vineyards, plantations
	and wineries
Photographer:	Virginia del Giudice

Haras Tres Pinos

Interior designer	Juan Ricci
Opening date:	1994
Address:	General Rodriguez, Buenos Aires. Argentina
	catballou@ciudad.com.ar
Rooms:	20 doubles
Services:	Restaurant, bar, meeting room, games, convention room
Special features:	Football and polo classes
Photographer:	Ricardo Labougle, Ana Cardinale

La Pascuala Delta Lodge

Opening Date:	2001
Address:	Delta del Rio Parana. Argentina
Tel.:	+ 54 11 4728 1253/1395
Fax:	+ 54 11 4728 1475/2070
	rhouston@infovia.com.ar
	www.lapascuala.com
Rooms:	15 individual bungalows
Services:	Restaurant, CD, air conditioning, heating, private terraces
Special features:	Fishing, kayaking, swimming, trekking, water sports, excursions.
Photographer:	Ricardo Labougle, Ana Cardinale

Posada La Bonita

INTERIOR DESIGNER:	Franco Martini
OPENING DATE:	1999
ADDRESS:	Parage el Soberbio
	Provincia de Misiones. Argentina
TEL.:	+ 54 3755 680 380
	www.posadalabonita.com.ar
ROOMS:	3 jungle huts
	www.posadalabonita.com.ar
SERVICES:	Horseback riding, kayaking, canoeing, excursions
	to waterfalls
PHOTOGRAPHER:	Virginia del Giudice

Hospedería Convento La Parra

ARCHITECT	(Rehabilitation) Francisco Viñao D´Lom
INTERIOR DESIGNER:	María Ulecia & Javier Muñoz
CONSTRUCTION DATE:	1673
OPENING DATE:	2000
ADDRESS:	Santa María, 16
	La Parra 06176, Badajoz. Spain
TEL.:	+34 924 682 692
FAX:	+34 924 682 619
	laparra@wanadoo.es
	www.laparra.net
ROOMS:	21
SERVICES:	Restaurant, convention room, swimming pool
SPECIAL FEATURES:	Gift shop, outdoor activities, cooking classes
PHOTOGRAPHER:	Pep Escoda

LINDOS HUÉSPEDES

INTERIOR DESIGNER:	Angeles G. Giró & Luis Vidal
OPENING DATE:	2000
ADDRESS:	Carretera de Pals
	Torroella de Montgrí, Girona. Spain
TEL./FAX:	+ 34 972 66 82 03
	lindoshuespedes@yahoo.es
ROOMS:	6 doubles and 1 suite
SERVICES:	Restaurant, terraces over the river, gardens
SPECIAL FEATURES:	Excursions, beach and golf course close
PHOTOGRAPHER:	Pere Planells

RESERVA ROTANA

CONSTRUCTION DATE:	1996
ADDRESS:	Camí de S'Avall, Km 3
	07500 Manacor, Mallorca. Spain
TEL.:	+ 34 971 551 838
FAX:	+ 34 971 555 258
	info@reservarotana.com
	www.reservarotana.com
ROOMS:	21
SERVICES:	Minibar, satellite TV, air conditioning, heating
SPECIAL FEATURES:	Wine cellar
PHOTOGRAPHER:	Pep Escoda

HOTEL LES TERRASSES

OWNER AND CREATOR:	Françoise Pialoux
OPENING DATE:	1989
ADDRESS:	Can Vich, Carretera de Santa Eulalia, Km 1
	Ibiza. Spain
TEL./FAX :	+ 34 971 33 2643
	info@lesterrasses.net
	www.lesterrasses.net
ROOMS:	8 doubles
SERVICES:	Restaurant, satellite TV, air conditioning, heating,
	two swimming pools, garden, tennis court
SPECIAL FEATURES:	Beach and golf course nearby
PHOTOGRAPHER:	Pere Planells

La Fuente de la Higuera

Construction date:	18th century
Opening date	1999
Address:	Partido de los Frontones
	29400 Ronda, Málaga. Spain
Tel.:	+ 34 952 11 43 55
Fax:	+ 34 952 11 43 56
	info@hotellafuente.com
	www.hotellafuente.com
Rooms:	10, including one apartment
Services:	Internet, TV, Hifi, library, central heating
Special features:	Trekking, mountainbiking, kayaking and canoeing
Photographer:	Ricardo Labougle, Victor Carro

Hotel Son Gener

ARCHITECT:	Antonio Esteva
OPENING DATE:	1998
ADDRESS:	Carretera Son Cervera-Artà, Km 3
	Son Cervera, 07550 Mallorca. Spain
TEL.:	+ 34 971 1836 12
FAX:	+ 34 971 1835 91
ROOMS:	10 junior suites
SERVICES:	Restaurant, bar, phone, fax, air conditioning,
	swimming pool
SPECIAL FEATURES:	Beach and golf course nearby
PHOTOGRAPHER:	Pere Planells

Hotel Casablanca

Architect:	Domingo Fernandez Lorencio
Interior designer:	Susan Craig Dring
Construction date:	18th century
Opening date:	1997
Address:	Teodoro Molina, 12
	29480 Gaucín, Málaga. Spain
Tel./Fax:	+34 95 215 10 19
	dring@mercuryin.es
Rooms:	8
Services:	Restaurant
Special features:	Garden, swimming pool, panoramic views of the Mediterranean and Africa
Photographer:	Ricardo Labougle, Victor Carro

Ca's Xorc

ARCHITECT:	Wolfgang Nikolaus Schmidt, Juan Puigserver, Mariano Barceló
OPENING DATE:	2000
ADDRESS:	Carretera de Deià, Km 56,1 07100 Soller, Mallorca. Spain
TEL.:	+ 34 971 638 091
FAX:	+ 34 971 632 949 stay@casxorc.com www.casxorc.com
ROOMS:	10 doubles
SERVICES:	Restaurant, bar, internet, swimming pool, gardens
SPECIAL FEATURES:	Convention room with audio/visual equipment, jacuzzi, sauna and steam bath
PHOTOGRAPHER:	Pep Escoda

Residencia Casa Pagès "El Folló"

Interior design:	By the owners
Opening date:	1993
Address:	08593 Tagamanent, Barcelona. Spain
Tel.:	+ 34 93 842 91 16
	www.elfollo.com
Rooms:	8 doubles
Services:	Heating, restaurant serves organic food from the region
Special features:	Cooking classes, horseback riding (no beginners)

Hospedería Parque de Monfragüe

ARCHITECT	Manuel Jaureguibeitia
INTERIOR DESIGN:	Manuel Jaureguibeitia
CONSTRUCTION DATE:	1999
ADDRESS:	Carretera Plasencia-Trujillo, Km 39,1
	10694 Torrejón el Rubio, Cáceres. Spain
TEL.:	+ 34 927 455 245
FAX:	+ 34 927 455 016
	hotel@hotelmonfrague.com
	www.hotelmonfrague.com
ROOMS:	48 doubles
SERVICES:	Restaurant, bar-café, Hifi, TV, phone, minibar, heating, laundry, terrace with view, meeting room
SPECIAL FEATURES:	Barbecue, lounge with chimney, swimming pool, excursions and adventure sports, contemporary art-collection, designer furniture
PHOTOGRAPHER:	Pep Escoda

Bali Spirit Hotel and Spa

Owner:	IB. Tantra
Designer:	IB. Tantra
Opening date:	1997, amplification 2000
Address:	189, Nyuh Kuning
	Ubud, Bali 80571. Indonesia
Tel.:	+ 62 361 974013
Fax:	+ 62 361 974012
	info@balispirithotel.com
	www.balispirithotel.com
Rooms:	19 private suites and villas
Services:	Restaurant, bar, air conditioning, phone
Special features:	Hot water garden showers, massage and spa
	treatments, cultural programs, free chauffer service
Photographer:	Anom Manik Agung

Hotel Nour el Qurna

Owner:	Mahmoud
Opening date:	1997
Address:	Luxor-Qurna
	West Bank, Luxor. Egypt
Tel.:	+ 20 95 311 430
Rooms:	8 doubles
Services:	Restaurant with Egyptian and European cuisine, air conditioning, heating, swimming pool
Special features:	Located in the Valley of the Queens
Photographer:	Ricardo Labougle, Hugo Curletto

HOTEL MARSAM

OPENING DATE:	1998
ADDRESS:	Nour el Qurna
	West Bank, Luxor. Egypt
TEL.:	+ 20 95 372 403
ROOMS:	24 doubles
SERVICES:	Restaurant with Egyptian and European cuisine, air conditioning; heating
SPECIAL FEATURES:	An early century refuge for American archeologists converted into a hotel and still visited by archeologists from all over the world
PHOTOGRAPHER:	Ricardo Labougle. Hugo Curletto

La Saracina

OPENING DATE: 1991
ADDRESS: S. S. 146, Km 29
700 Pienza, Siena. Italy
TEL.: + 39 0578 748 022
FAX: + 39 0578 748 018
www.lasaracina.it
ROOMS: 3 suites, 2 doubles, 1 apartment
SERVICES: Breakfast, TV, minibar, fireplaces
SPECIAL FEATURES: Swimming pool, tennis court, jacuzzi, garden
PHOTOGRAPHER: Pep Escoda

TENUTA SAN VITO

OPENING DATE:	1985
ADDRESS:	Via San Vito, 32-I
	50056 Montelupo Fiorentino, Florence. Italy
TEL.:	+ 39 0571 51411
FAX:	+ 39 0571 51405
	sanvito@san-vito.com
	www.san-vito.com
ROOMS:	4 apartments/villas
SERVICES:	Fireplace, private terraces, meeting lounge, swimming pool
SPECIAL FEATURES:	Weekly wine-tasting, mountain bikes
PHOTOGRAPHER:	Pep Escoda

Torre di Bellosguardo

OWNER:	Amerigo Franchetti
INTERIOR DESIGNER:	Amerigo Franchetti
OPENING DATE:	1996
ADDRESS:	Via Roti Michelozzi 2
	50124 Florence. Italy
TEL.:	+ 39 055 229 8145
FAX:	+ 39 055 229 008
	info@torrebellosguardo.com
	www.torrebellosguardo.com
ROOMS:	8 doubles, 7 suites, 1 single
SERVICES:	Breakfast, bar, internet, laundry, swimming pool
SPECIAL FEATURES:	Sports center, sauna, massage, flower garden,
	vegetable garden, vineyard, olive groves
PHOTOGRAPHER:	Pep Escoda

BAIA BENIAMIN

INTERIOR DESIGNER:	Mr. Brunelli
CONSTRUCTION DATE:	1986
ADDRESS:	Corso Europa, 63
	Grimaldi Inferiore, Ventimiglia. Italy
TEL.:	+ 39 018 438 002
FAX:	+ 39 018 438 027
	baiabeniamin@libero.it
	www.baiabeniamin.it
ROOMS:	5 doubles
SERVICES:	Restaurant, bar, phone, TV, air conditioning, safe,
	minibar, breakfast on the terrace
SPECIAL FEATURES:	Wine cellar, terrace to the bay, private beach
PHOTOGRAPHER:	Pep Escoda

TENUTA LE VISTE

INTERIOR DESIGNER:	Rodolfo Bartoli
OPENING DATE:	1996
ADDRESS:	Via del Leone 11
	50028 Mosciano-Scandicci. Italy
TEL.:	+ 39 055 768 543
FAX:	+ 39 055 768 531
	birgiter@tin.it
ROOMS:	4 doubles
SERVICES:	Satellite TV, air conditioning, mini bar, antique furniture
SPECIAL FEATURES:	Huge park with olive trees and swimming pool, own oil production
PHOTOGRAPHER:	Pep Escoda

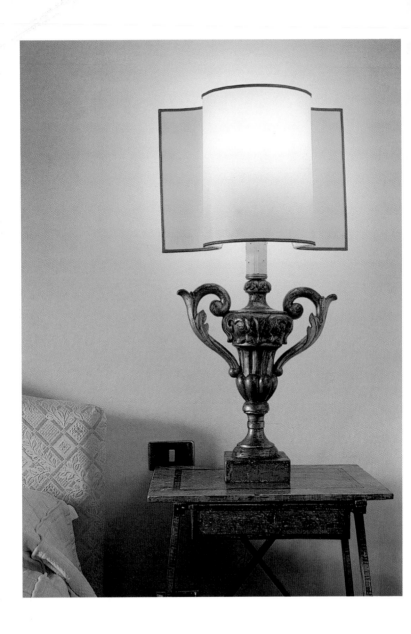

HOTEL FONTELUNGA

INTERIOR DESIGNER:	Philip Robinson
OPENING DATE:	2000
ADDRESS:	Via Cunicchio n° 5
	Foiano della Chiana, 52045 Arezzo. Italy
TEL.:	+ 39 0575 660 410
FAX:	+ 39 0575 661 963
	sales@tuscanholiday.com
	www.tuscanholiday.com
ROOMS:	8 doubles, 1 twin
SERVICES:	Continental breakfast, CD, phone, air conditioning,
	laundry, modern en-suite showers and bathrooms
SPECIAL FEATURES:	Swimming pool
PHOTOGRAPHER:	Pep Escoda

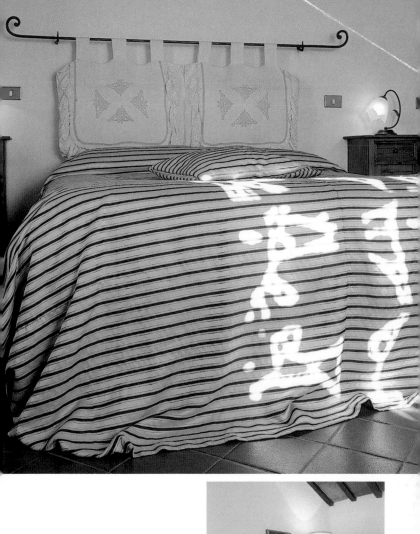

Hotel Villa Fiesole

Architect:	Bianchini
Interior designer:	Bianchini
Opening date:	1995
Address:	Via Beato Angélico, 35
	50014 Florence. Italy
Tel.:	+ 39 055 597 252
Fax:	+ 39 055 599 133
	villafiesole@hotmail.com
Rooms:	28 doubles
Services:	Restaurant, bar, internet, cable TV, laundry
Special features:	Massage
Photographer:	Pep Escoda

L'Oustau de Beaumanière

CONSTRUCTION DATE:	15th Century
OPENING DATE:	1945
ADDRESS:	13520 Les Baux de Provence. France
TEL.:	+ 33 490 54 33 07
FAX:	+ 33 490 54 40 46
	contact@oustaudebaumaniere.com
	www.oustaudebaumaniere.com
ROOMS:	27 doubles, including apartments
SERVICES:	Mini bar, TV, air conditioning, swimming pool
SPECIAL FEATURES:	Breakfast on the terrace, pick-up service, tennis court, heliport, golf course and horseback riding close
PHOTOGRAPHER:	Pere Planells

L'Oustau de Beaumanière **373**

Chambre de Séjour avec Vue

Designers:	Pierre Jacaud & Kamila Regent
Opening date:	1996
Address:	Rue de la Bourgade
	84400 Saignon. France
Tel./Fax:	+33 4900 48501
	chambreavecvue@vox-pop.net
	www.chambreavecvue.com
Rooms:	4 rooms and 2 apartments
Services:	Restaurant, bar, lounge rooms
Special features:	Sculpture park, art gallery
Photographer:	Pere Planells

LA PAULINE

OWNERS:	Ita & Regis Macquet
CONSTRUCTION DATE:	Late 18th century
OPENING DATE:	1998
ADDRESS:	Les Pinchinats
	Chemin de la Fontaine des Tuiles
	13100 Aix-en-Provence. France
TEL.:	+ 33 442 170 260
FAX:	+ 33 442 170 261
	la-pauline@wanadoo.fr
	www.la-pauline.com
ROOMS:	4 doubles and 1 suite
SERVICES:	Restaurant, bar, phone, fax, breakfast,
	air conditioning, heating
SPECIAL FEATURES:	Historical 18th century gardens
PHOTOGRAPHER:	Pere Planells

LA BASTIDE DE CAPELONGUE

OWNERS:	Loubet family
ADDRESS:	Bastide de Capelongue
	84480 Bonnieux en Provence. France
TEL.:	+ 33 490 758 978
FAX:	+ 33 490 759 303
	bastide@francemarket.com
	www.francemarket.com/capelongue
ROOMS:	17 doubles
SERVICES:	Air conditioning, swimming pool
SPECIAL FEATURES:	French cuisine prepared with vegetables from the own garden or from the region
PHOTOGRAPHER:	Ricardo Labougle, Victor Carro